Eight Little Organ Preludes and

Johann Sebastian Bach
Transcribed for Piano by
Frederick C. Schreiber

1

Prelude
Allegro moderato

Piano

46237cx

4

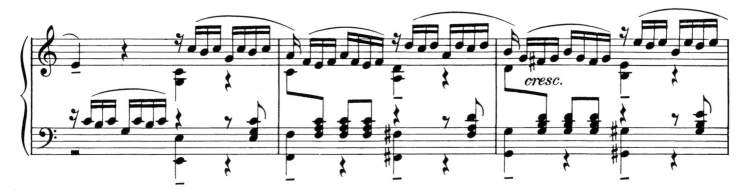

46237

Fugue

6

2

Prelude
Moderato

Fugue
Andante

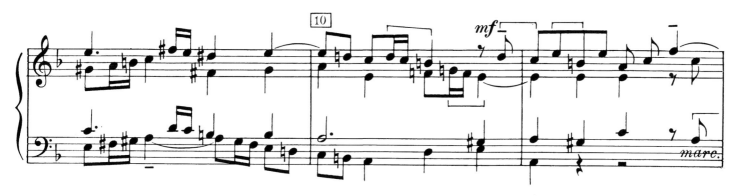

3

Prelude
Grave

Fugue

Andante

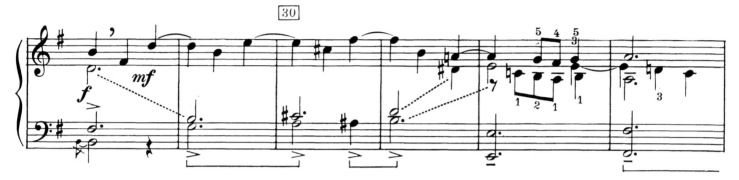

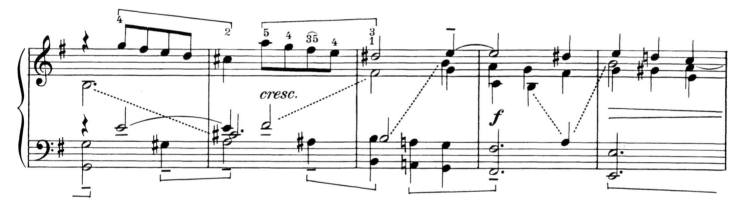

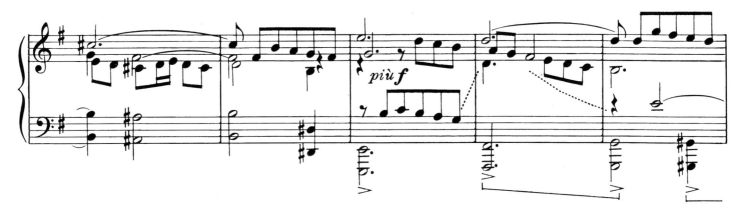

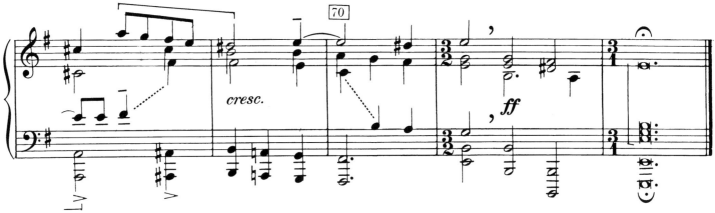

4

Prelude
Andantino

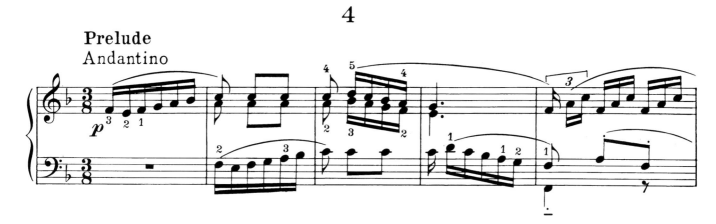

poco a poco cresc.

poco a poco cresc.

Fugue

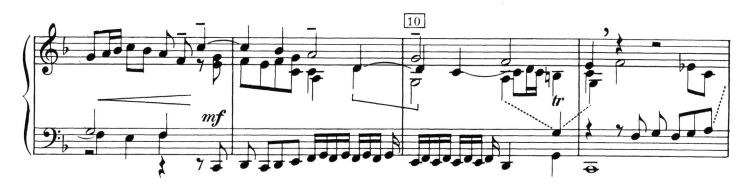

5

Prelude

Grave

Poco più mosso

Fugue
Moderato

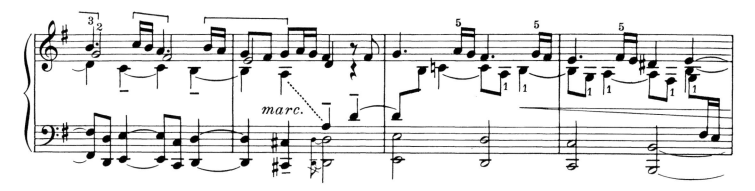

6

Prelude

Moderato

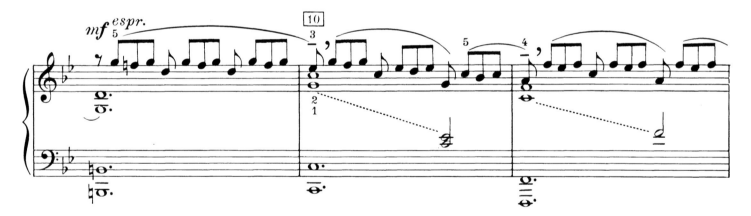

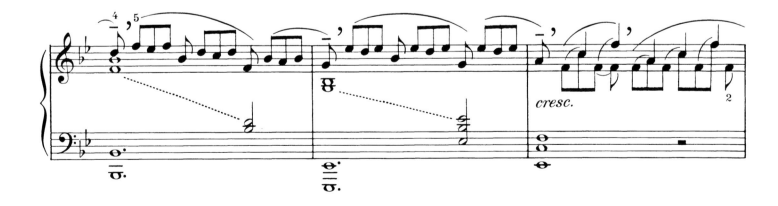

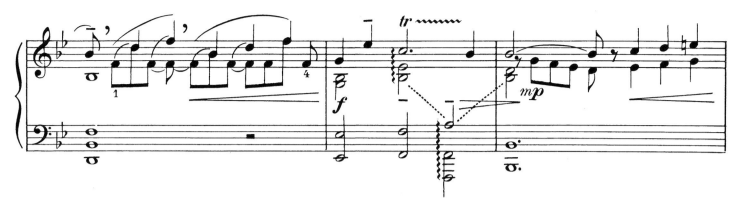

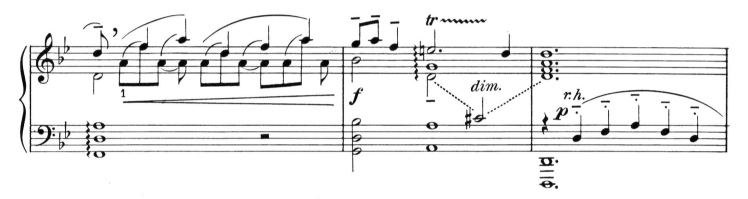

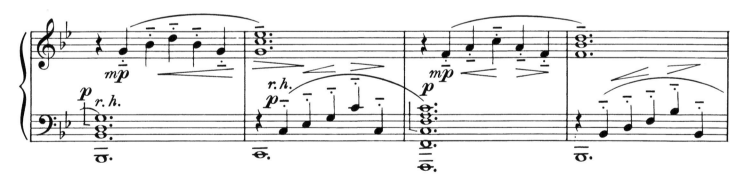

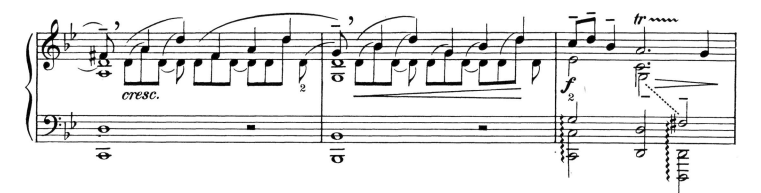

Fugue
Moderato

poco *f*

cresc.

20

f *p* *f* *p*

mp

mf

7

Prelude
Allegro moderato

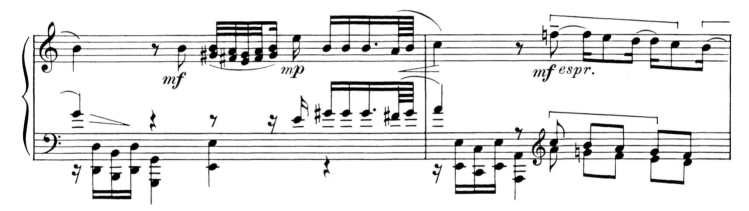

Fugue

Andante

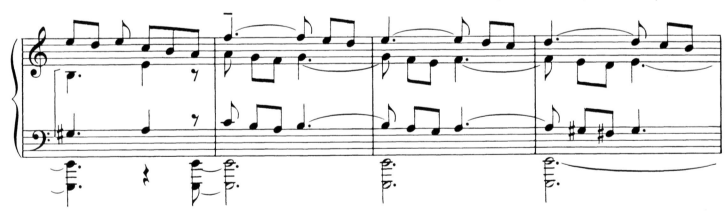

8

Prelude
Allegro

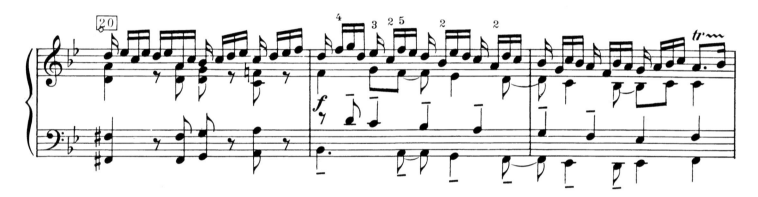

Fugue

Allegro moderato

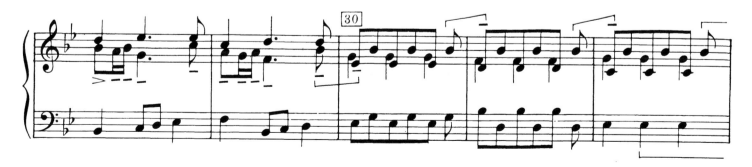